ECHOES OF THE HEART

Echoes of the Heart

MAXI JAFFE

CONTENTS

1	Beatles	1
2	Only 49 Days	2
3	I Cry	3
4	Don't Let Them Rule Your Life	4
5	Until We Meet Again	5
6	Something More	6
7	Crossed the Line	7
8	Long-legged Martini 1	8
9	Long-legged Martini 2	9
10	The Feisty One	10
11	More to Life	11
12	Just Screw It	12
13	The Struggle of Time	13
14	The Truth of Life and Love	14

15	Deepest Darkest Secrets	15
16	Sleepless Night	16
17	The Endless Cycle	17
18	The World of Colors	18
19	The Circle of Us	19
20	The Surrender of Longing	20
21	Wish for Failures	21
22	Prayer for Our Insanity	22
23	The Question	23
24	The Path Unknown	24
25	Bound By Love	25
26	Wings of Waiting	26
27	The Ides of March	27
28	The Games of Time	28
29	The Uncertainty of Me	29
30	The Struggle for Self	30
31	The Divine Within	31
32	A Real Dance	32
33	The Infinite Self	33
34	Reality of Forever	34

35	Just For You	35
36	The Key	36
37	Tick of The Clock	37
38	Through Your Eyes	38
39	Thunder and Lightning	39
40	My Smiley Butterfly Fly Friend	40
41	Rapunzel	41
42	Smart Ass of Compassion	42
43	Sue and Shoot	43
44	The Fat Cat's Hat	44
45	Webs of Treachery	45
46	The Gift of Forgiveness	46
47	Never and Always	47
48	The Duality of Love	48
49	Gingerbread Man	49

| 1 |

Beatles

Michelle, please help me, I can get by with a little help from my friends from all across the universe. Yesterday was the day to hide out in the yellow submarine from the octopus's garden. Today is the day to dance in the strawberry fields forever because we all need help. Happiness is a warm gun and so is revolution, because something in the way she moves makes it seem like I want you, I wanna hold your hand, and that all you need is love so let it be.

| 2 |

Only 49 Days

We're having fun. It doesn't hurt. We're speeding, laughing, and not caring about the future. Then Bam!, we're hit. It hurts like hell. We're lying on the ground, in a puddle of blood, hearing our parents' sobbing. In the distance, the chuckle of the devil is heard, visions of Moses, Jesus and Muhammad looking disappointed, while Buddha is chanting 49 days, only 49 days. We're confused, it wasn't supposed to end up like this, but it did, we're done, it's over, we're dead.

| 3 |

I Cry

I cry all day. I cry all night.
I cry in the darkness. I cry in the light.
I am so sad from this day on.
I cried an ocean because I'm so sad.
I smile all day. I smile all night.
I smile in the darkness. I smile in the light.
I am so happy from this day on.
I smiled a lot because I'm so happy.

| 4 |

Don't Let Them Rule Your Life

Does it matter that they care
Who you like or what you wear
Does it say anything that they hate
What you are or who you date
How do they not see
That who you are sets you free
How can they take away your rights
And expect you to give up without a fight
Why do they care about you
When your life does not affect what they do
Why do they have the say
In how you live and spend your day
Don't let them rule your life
And decide who is your husband or wife
Be confident, don't you see
Stand up to them and say I am me

5

Until We Meet Again

He is gone, but we will not forget him. Let his heart fly above the clouds to the place we go after. Let him see that our hearts are with him, but let him go on. For he has a purpose we know not of. Let us mourn for him, but also let us celebrate his life and honor his memory. We will miss you. Farewell, until we meet again.

| 6 |

Something More

How did this happen,
What did I do?
I thought it was fun
I really liked you.
It started with a kiss
And then we were on the floor,
It didn't end up like I planned
You wanted a lot more.
I didn't realize what was happening
Until it was too late,
It was all you ever wanted
It wasn't really a date.
I wasn't prepared
When you walked out the door,
I am very scared
And I'm lying on the floor.
Goodbye virginity
He took it and went away,
It wasn't the way I wanted
I thought he was here to stay.
But he's not here to stay
And he left me on the floor.
I know now that I am never
Going to want that "something more."

| 7 |

Crossed the Line

You said it would be fine
But you crossed the line.
You said it was just a kiss
And that it would not end up like this.
You said it wouldn't hurt
And after that I wouldn't feel like dirt.
You said it would feel good
But you knew it never would.
You said it was done and it was great
And the reason that we're together was fate.
I said that it was done and that you should pack
And that you should leave and never come back.
It is the end
I can't believe that you were my friend.
You said it would be fine
But it's not cause you crossed the line.

| 8 |

Long-legged Martini 1

I am many things, anything you want me to be,
A long-legged martini, a salsa dancer,
A sexy hot teacher in only black boots.
Whatever you want, I'll be.
If you only stop hitting me, I'll be fine.
Oh! You want me to be a hooker?
Ok, just don't make it hurt.
You want me to be a slutty teacher wearing only black boots?
That I can do.
Lie down and hold still?
Wait, that wasn't part of the plan.
Can I be your long-legged martini?
I really want to be your long-legged martini,
Please, it's better for me that way.

| 9 |

Long-legged Martini 2

I'm sorry I lied
Because I didn't want you to know that I cried
When you told me it was over for good
But I knew that it never would.
Please forgive me for all of this strife
You know that I have always wanted to be a part of your life
It doesn't matter that I'm your long-legged martini
Letting you love me in only boots and a bikini.
I am apologizing for all of my mistakes
And I'll beg and plead for as long as it takes
But you need to apologize for your mistakes too
For hurting me while all I did was love you
Forgiving me is your gift to me
Thank you for doing that, for setting me free.

| 10 |

The Feisty One

He could have been my brother,
The man I killed.
He could have been my lover
If he was more strong willed.
But all I saw was a pompous narcissistic fool
That grabbed my ass at the bar
I punched him and told him he was an arrogant tool
That should admire girls from afar.
But as he grabbed me and called me "the feisty one"
I jiu jitsued his ass to the floor.
I was walking away because I was done
When he pinned me to the door.
The surge of energy that enraged me made him fly across the room.
Red was all I could see, until I heard that boom.
Turning around, my heart stopped
At the sight of him on the floor.
All the rage dropped
And the red I saw was no more.
Cause he was dead
"The feisty one" was all he said.
He could have been my brother, or my lover
But he's not, and this remorse is all I've got.
The life that was lost could have been my family of friend
And I will remember him until the very end.

| 11 |

More to Life

Do I wake or do I sleep?
Is there reason for me to think?
About the things so deep
In my mind, written down with ink.
Should I live or should I die?
Is there reason for me to be alive?
When all I do is stay silent and lie,
Maybe it's time for me to say goodbye.
What if there is more to life?
Should I take that knife?
I want to get rid of all the pain,
Maybe my death won't be in vain.
I say you'll be okay as you start to cry,
It's my time to leave, to go, to fly.

| 12 |

Just Screw It

Just screw it. Screw the fact that I am halfway across the country and you are dying. I will be there. Screw the fact that the doctors say that you will be dead before morning. Just keep fighting. Screw the fact that I used my entire last month's paycheck for a round trip ticket to see you for a few minutes. I don't care. Just keep fighting, I will be there. Screw the flight plan of 5 hours; I'll make it in 4. Screw the speed limit; I need to be there for you. I race up the stairs and sprint to your room, and hug you and cry as the constant rhythmic beeping turns into one long beep that makes my insides squirm. But it doesn't matter, I was here. I was here for you, and I held you in your final minutes. As you took your final breath, I was here, and that's all that matters.

| 13 |

The Struggle of Time

Everyday life passes by slowly
And sometimes is too hard to bare
Everyday life is a long never-ending story
Just waiting to be shared
Everyday life passes by quickly
And it is harder than going on forever
Everyday life is a killer
But we'll make it, as long as we're together

| 14 |

The Truth of Life and Love

Who said life is this easy
Because really, it isn't so
If it truly were easy
Then why would we need to grow
Why would we need the tools
To get through all the strife?
If it isn't true then we're the fools
Who complicate this life
Who needs love to get by
When solidarity and loneliness are okay
But we do need love, don't lie
It has always been that way
So embrace love and live for the future
For you never know when it will end
Just find love and you'll be sure
You'll be okay, my friend

| 15 |

Deepest Darkest Secrets

Hello there. Is anybody out there?
I feel a need to share my deepest darkest secrets,
That I actually really don't want to share.
Are you listening?
I hope so, no, actually I hope not.
Oh, I don't know.
Should I tell you or should I not?
I don't know.
Will you tell anyone? No! Really?
Oh! Well, I don't believe you.
Secrets are never kept quiet.
I guess I won't tell you
but I really do want to share.
Will you come back?
Yes, please do, no, never mind.
I don't want to share with you.

| 16 |

Sleepless Night

How can this be?
I do not feel like I am me
The pain is just too great
And I'm not sure I want to wait.
Let me go into the sleepless night
That will lessen my pain and cloud my sight
I'm not quitting, really, just taking a rest
That way after I can feel my best
But I'm not coming back, I'm letting go to fly
I'm sorry, forgive me, it's over, goodbye.

| 17 |

The Endless Cycle

Proud clouds sit high in the sky,
Wanting to rain, but it causes them pain.
Finally, the rain falls down to town,
The wind blows, as water flows,
Into oceans and streams,
Until the sun's beams
Turn the water into steam.
The steam rises back to the sky,
To the proud clouds that sigh,
Raining once more, in pain, down to town,
Flowing and going back to the stream,
Turning into steam again,
To form the proud clouds that rain in pain
Keeping the cycle going on forever and ever.

| 18 |

The World of Colors

Orange man is eating the green door.
Green man is furious.
Green man removes the red roof from the blue house.
Red and blue men are enraged.
Red and blue men take the yellow bed
and throw it into the purple ocean
which is actually the sun in disguise
as the World of Colors goes into World War 27
that this time might be the war
that actually makes a difference.

| 19 |

The Circle of Us

We are the compass, I, the soul fixed foot,
Do not move to stir for you.
You, the other foot, run around me, roaming far,
But always coming back to me.
My firmness makes thy circle just
And makes you end where you began.
Together we are one.

The Surrender of Longing

Care less eyes, lips, and hands to miss,
Close, dear eyes, and cease thy quest for bliss.
Lips, be still; no longer seek what's mine.
Hands, rest gently—halt your eager climb.
Care less eyes, lips, and hands to miss,
Release your longing; fade into abyss.

| 21 |

Wish for Failures

Why does it happen that everything we ask for we never get, and what we get we never ask for? Why is it that we always seem to get lucky with the "failures?" We always ask to ace the test or for it to be a sunny day but, like always, its turns out to be a crappy day and you epically failed the test. Let's, for once, wish for all the "failures", for everything we don't want, that way, when we don't get lucky, we will.

| 22 |

Prayer for Our Insanity

Our God and God of our ancestors: We ask Your blessings for our craziness, for our foolishness, for our level minded stupidity and for all who exercise a lack of common sense. Teach us insights of Your irrational experiences, that we may administer all unwise affairs of state unfairly, that insanity and madness, stupidity and absurdity, idiocy and ridiculousness may forever abide in our midst. Creator of all foolhardy behavior, bless all of our craziness with Your spirit. Give us leave of our sanity, for if we have it we are boring. Let us have the ability to embrace the lunacy and throw away our logic. May this land under Your outrageous oversight be an influence for all satirical realities throughout the world uniting all people in irony and craziness and helping them to fulfill the vision of Your absurd lunacy: "Insanity shall not go against the craziness of lunacy, neither shall they experience good judgment any more." And let us say: Amen.

| 23 |

The Question

As I dance in the acid rain I ponder this question as my skin starts to boil and slide off. On the ground, in a pile of skin, bones and blood, I am reformed, but only on the condition of not pondering this question. Don't you see that this question doesn't have an answer and that as you ponder it, it consumes and destroys you. Newly formed and doing anything to not think of the question, I dance away only to ponder the question once more and crash to the floor in a pile of skin and bones. I shouldn't have pondered the question. But where'd the blood go?

| 24 |

The Path Unknown

This shaking keeps me steady
For I do not know if I am ready
I wake to sleep and take my waking slow
Yet where I'm bound, I do not know
God bless the ground below me
Cause it's the only thing keeping me free
I learn by going where I have to go
But where I'm going, I may never know

| 25 |

Bound By Love

You
The song inside my head.
The words waiting to be said.
Longing to break free.
You
The love of my life. I dream to be your wife. Always in your arms
Me
The one who longs for you.
Do you long for me too?
The question waiting for an answer.
Me
Always held within your heart.
I long for you when we're apart.
Together at last.
You and me
Two peas in a pod. Like earth and god. Together forever.
Me and you
Like gravity always there.
Bound by love and tender care.
Finally, able to show love.
You
Like the sun on a rainy day.
But rain is good, okay?
Now, able to shine.

| 26 |

Wings of Waiting

Time has come today
To make me fly away
But the sky objects.
Rain falls through the trees
I see clouds through the leaves
I want to fly but can't.
My wings are damp and wet
I can only wait and regret
The fact that I can't escape.
My time has come to fly
The rain has stopped, goodbye.

| 27 |

The Ides of March

The Ides of March is approaching
Beware and be ready
The Ideas of March is approaching
Strong and steady
It is a day to fear
Everywhere, far and near
It's not a day to dwell on
You don't want it to be here
But it is coming again
Like the sunrise every day
At least we are not Caesar
So we do not have to stay away
Because when Brutus plunged the fatal blow
Caesar fell to the floor
At least we are safe
Because it is a day and nothing more

| 28 |

The Games of Time

There are places in the world where time stops,
And everything ceases to matter.
There are places where things happen that we can't understand.
In the real world, time takes pleasure in kicking our asses.
Time loves to play games with us
Slowing down or speeding up,
Right when we don't want it to.
Time is everything we don't want it to be:
Slow, fast, or stopped
When all we want is to be anywhere but here.
In the end, all we can say is…
Time sucks.

| 29 |

The Uncertainty of Me

I am me
But I don't know what I'm meant to be
Or what to do
And I don't know if I want to be with you
Or with the other guy
But I don't want to be alone when I die
Or in life
And I'm not sure I want to be your wife
Or anyone's at all
But I guess I'm going to try or else I'm going to fall

| 30 |

The Struggle for Self

Hello my friends,
Can we meet before it ends?
I'd like to talk about who I may be
For I'm unsure if it's truly me
Let's discuss the forces at play,
That cloud our minds, leading us astray.
Is it the divine spirit that strengthens our souls
Or the satanic devil that shatters our goals
Whatever it is, fight with all your might,
And never forget to guard the light.
For one day, we will be free,
To shout and declare, I am me.

| 31 |

The Divine Within

You are who you are, you are free
Everything bad is over, it's done
Now it's time to be good and have fun
And be whoever you want to be
Look out across the endless blue sea
It's not a lake, it's vast and wide,
It will always be there, you cannot hide
Watch it twist and turn, you know it is She
God is everywhere, remember She can hear
She hears you there; She knows your thought
She's not just a person, but divine,
Always divine, all year, all time.
Just remember you will be fine
As long as you're here, but you're not.

32

A Real Dance

Today is the day to dance
Please, take a chance
Dance a real dance, it's fun
Don't worry, it's almost done
Take the time to be with me
Don't be scared, don't you see
Life is short, it's now or never
Let's dance this dance, together forever.

| 33 |

The Infinite Self

It takes something big to make time stop
And this is big, as he throws the dart
It hits my forehead, then I drop
Piercing my brain and breaking my heart
Time is gone, but I will be alive forever
My body has no limits, I am free
To be anything I want, it's now or never
I can be anything and everything, as long as it's me.
It takes time, but now I know
I can be anything, nothing, I can shrink or grow
I can change my face, my voice, my hair
I can disappear, be here or nowhere
It's all I ever wanted, to reach this state
To be whatever I choose, with this newfound trait.
I'll go experiment, to truly be me,
Leaving forever, always bound to be free.

| 34 |

Reality of Forever

Life is too fast. Everything moves in slow motion,
Then speeds up to double time when something important begins.
It's time to take a break.
Let's lie on sunny beaches,
Watching blue-footed boobies dance in the air,
Or safari through Africa's chaotic jungles,
Hunting the Big Five.
Maybe we'll jump off a bridge or two,
Or venture to Asia,
Walk the Great Wall of China,
And attempt to climb Mount Everest,
Only to fail miserably.
But then, time speeds up again,
And we're back to the reality of forever.

| 35 |

Just For You

I want you to know I wrote this poem just for you. I chose the name just for you, the ***font***, the   s p a c i n g, everything.

Look how I

skip from one

line to

another. Look at my CApiTalS anywhere or ALWAYS.

This is a poem JusT foR YoU. I bordered it just for you. I changed color just for you. Look at this

amazing poem I wrote

       JUsT fOr yOU.

| 36 |

The Key

The key to my heart lies at the end of this treasure map.
Get to the end, and I'm all yours.
It begins with a map of a body of water,
No directions—yet you find it.
Damn.
It's a small lake, in the middle of nowhere, Kansas.
The next map leads you to a jungle in the Andes,
Atop a mountain that demands a seven-hour hike each way.
Shit.
Then, to a snowcap in Antarctica,
Thirty below, at the center of the South Pole.
Next, it takes you to the top of Mount Everest,
But still, you make it.
Uh oh.
Then, a pride of lions in Africa,
The map clutched in their jaws,
But you wrestle it free anyway.
Finally, you reach the Eiffel Tower,
Ripped clothes, shaggy hair
And tell me you love me.
Maybe… maybe you are worth it?

| 37 |

Tick of The Clock

The tick of the clock
And the closed lock
On the door
That leaves you wanting more
Open it up for us to see
Do it now, do it for me
Love me now, don't wait till the end
I want to be more than just your friend
But with the tick of the clock
The mind will lock
Love will be lost
And our happiness is the cost

| 38 |

Through Your Eyes

I don't know what to do
I want to see myself the way you do.
Through your eyes, the view is clear,
But mine are clouded by doubt and fear.
How you see me
Is how I long to be.
Realization is the start
But it is only just a part.
Confidence is the key
To who I want to be.
And that is me.

| 39 |

Thunder and Lightning

Don't let the lightning overcome you.
Fight it, fight it for all its worth.
Instead, let the thunder overcome you,
For sound has no control upon a person.
Hear the thunder, watch the lightning,
For you never know when it will come back again.

| 40 |

My Smiley Butterfly Fly Friend

You will never wear a crazy pretend moist cat bounce dream
Like a played bluff of silly monkey feline,
From post-vacation liquidness in this funny yellow ocean
My smiley butterfly-fly friend,
Thus, with only a sad street couch,
Anyone leaping with joy can dance and sing over my moon.

| 41 |

Rapunzel

Rapunzel, Rapunzel, let down your hair!
Why?
Will it hurt?
Will my hair withstand the pressure?
Did you wash your hands?
Is this the only way up?
And what exactly are you going to do once you get up here?

| 42 |

Smart Ass of Compassion

You are mine, but don't forget to be nice.
I know you're not the tiny tiger of integrity,
Nor the smart ass of compassion,
But you are the little lion man of Crazy Oz Land,
An integral part of my sanity.
So remember, be kind, rewind.

| 43 |

Sue and Shoot

Shelly sued Sara so Sara shot Shelly and Shelly showed Sara that Sara should shoot shots sooner and straighter.

| 44 |

The Fat Cat's Hat

The fat cat at bat with a hat sat flat on a mat
while the rat, the brat and the gnat chat about
the fat cat that sat splat on a mat at bat with a hat.

| 45 |

Webs of Treachery

Behold the god-taker, maker, breaker,
Dreams ensnared in webs of treachery,
Weaving through proudly proclaimed party lines.

| 46 |

The Gift of Forgiveness

When given forgiveness, it's never fast,
It takes time for it to truly last.
It is something earned, to be forgiven
Forgiveness can't be spelled without given

| 47 |

Never and Always

Never say never
Always say always
Nothing is unreachable
And everything is achievable

| 48 |

The Duality of Love

Love is a clever thing
Sneaking up when you're not looking
But when your heart's desire is not searching,
Love becomes an evil thing.

| 49 |

Gingerbread Man

Not the gumdrop button!
The gingerbread man pleaded,
Anything but that!
Take my arm, my chocolate frosting hair,
Anything but that.
Take my gingerbread house,
My gingerbread car,
But not the gumdrop button!

www.ingramcontent.com/pod-product-compliance
Lightning Source LLC
LaVergne TN
LVHW020427070526
838199LV00004B/313